SCIENCE EXPLORER

LEVERS AND PULLEYS

SUPER COOL
SCIENCE
EXPERIMENTS:
LEVERS AND
PULLEYS

by Dana Meachen Rau

CHERRY LAKE PUBLISHING • ANN ARBOR, MICHIGAN

A NOTE TO PARENTS AND TEACHERS: Please review the instructions for these experiments before your children do them. Be sure to help them with any experiments you do not think they can safely conduct on their own.

A NOTE TO KIDS: Be sure to ask an adult for help with these experiments when you need it. Always put your safety first!

Published in the United States of America by
Cherry Lake Publishing
Ann Arbor, Michigan
www.cherrylakepublishing.com

Content Editor: Robert Wolffe, EdD,
Professor of Teacher Education,
Bradley University, Peoria, Illinois

Book design and illustration: The Design Lab

Photo Credits: Cover and page 1, ©Oreundici/Dreamstime.com; page 4, ©Pichugin Dmitry, used under license from Shutterstock, Inc.; page 12, ©Mcininch/Dreamstime.com; page 14, ©dragon_fang, used under license from Shutterstock, Inc.; page 15, ©Olivier Asselin/Alamy; page 19, ©Henry Westheim Photography/Alamy; page 24, ©Paulacobleigh/Dreamstime.com; page 28, ©iStockphoto.com/LeggNet

Library of Congress Cataloging-in-Publication Data
Rau, Dana Meachen, 1971–
  Super cool science experiments: Levers and pulleys / by Dana Meachen Rau.
      p. cm.—(Science explorer)
  Includes bibliographical references and index.
  ISBN-13: 978-1-60279-537-2   ISBN-10: 1-60279-537-1 (lib. bdg.)
  ISBN-13: 978-1-60279-616-4   ISBN-10: 1-60279-616-5 (pbk.)
  1. Levers—Experiments—Juvenile literature. 2. Pulleys—Experiments—Juvenile literature. I. Title. II. Series.
  TJ147.R36 2010
  621.8078—dc22   2009002699

Cherry Lake Publishing would like to acknowledge the work of The Partnership for 21st Century Skills. Please visit www.21stcenturyskills.org for more information.

SCIENCE EXPLORER

LEVERS AND PULLEYS

TABLE OF CONTENTS

Need a Lift?

Do you think ancient Egyptians used levers to build this?

They do all sorts of jobs. They make our lives easier. What are they? Levers and pulleys! People have been using levers and pulleys for thousands of years. Some experts even think that levers and pulleys may have helped ancient Egyptians build the pyramids. Levers and pulleys are simple machines. They are very helpful tools.

Science is at work every time levers and pulleys do their jobs. In this book, we'll learn how scientists think. We'll do that by experimenting with levers and pulleys. Would you believe that you can do experiments with supplies you already have at home? Don't forget the best part: we'll have fun and learn new things along the way!

First Things First

Scientists learn by studying things very carefully. For example, scientists who focus on levers and pulleys think about how objects move. They test different ways to lift objects, and they experiment to see how levers and pulleys can make lifting easier.

Good scientists write down their observations. Sometimes those observations lead scientists to ask new questions. With new questions in mind, they design experiments to find the answers.

When scientists plan experiments, they must think very clearly. The way they think about problems is often called the scientific method. What is the scientific method? It's a step-by-step way of finding answers to specific questions. The steps don't always follow the same pattern. Sometimes scientists change their minds. The process often works something like this:

Scientists take notes to record each step.

5

- **Step One:** A scientist gathers all the facts and makes observations about one particular thing.
- **Step Two:** The scientist comes up with a question that is not answered by all the observations and facts.
- **Step Three:** The scientist creates a hypothesis. This is a statement of what the scientist thinks is probably the answer to the question.
- **Step Four:** The scientist tests the hypothesis. He or she designs an experiment to see whether the hypothesis is correct. The scientist does the experiment and writes down what happens.
- **Step Five:** The scientist draws a conclusion based on how the experiment turned out. The conclusion might be that the hypothesis is correct. Sometimes, though, the hypothesis is not correct. In that case, the scientist might develop a new hypothesis and another experiment.

In the following experiments, we'll see the scientific method in action. First, we'll gather some facts and observations about levers and pulleys. For each experiment, we'll also develop a question and a hypothesis. Next, we'll do the experiment to see if our hypothesis is correct. By the end of the experiment, we should know something new about levers and pulleys. Scientists, are you ready? Then let's get started!

Experiment #1

Move Your

Fulcrum

and Save

Money!

Did you know that a playground seesaw is a kind of lever? In this experiment, we'll build a smaller version of a see-saw with an empty thread spool, 2 cups, a ruler, and some pennies. As you are doing the experiment, keep in mind that a lever has 3 parts. The load is the object you are trying to lift. In this case, our load will be 5 pennies in a cup. The effort is the force you use to push down on the other end of the ruler to lift the pennies. In this experiment, the effort will also be pennies. The spool will act as the fulcrum, the part of the lever that does not move.

So, how much effort do you think we need to lift 5 pennies off of a tabletop? Again, picture a seesaw on the playground. The seesaw would be balanced if 2 children of the same weight sat on each end. Each child would also have to sit the same distance from the fulcrum.

At this point, you may be asking yourself the following questions: Will the lever be balanced if there is an equal number of pennies on each side? What if there is a smaller number of pennies on the effort side? What if there is a greater number of pennies on the effort side? Let's test this hypothesis: **To balance a 5-penny load, you will need an effort made up of at least 5 pennies.**

Here's what you'll need:
- A small, empty thread spool
- Some masking tape
- 2 small paper cups, labeled Cup #1 and Cup #2
- A 12-inch (30.5 centimeter) ruler
- 30 pennies

This is all you need to experiment with a lever!

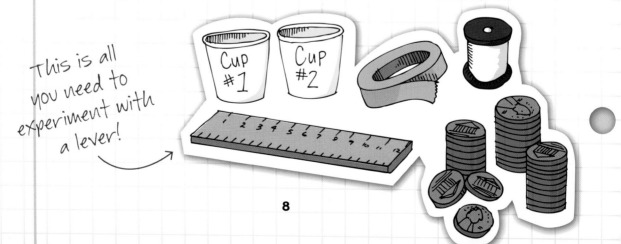

load

effort

Cup #1

Cup #2

fulcrum

Instructions:

1. Lay the spool horizontally on a tabletop so that it would roll if you pushed it. Tape the spool to the tabletop so that it doesn't move.

2. Place the 2 cups facedown on the table, with Cup #1 on the left and Cup #2 on the right. Lay the ruler across them so that the ruler numbers are facing down. Make sure the cups are as close to each end of the ruler as possible, then tape each end of the ruler to the bottom of each cup.

3. Turn the ruler over (with the cups attached and facing up on either end). Then place the ruler across the spool. The spool should be under the 6-inch (15.2 cm) mark on the ruler.

4. Put 5 pennies into Cup #1. This is the lever's load. Try your best to place the pennies in the center of the cup. Then start adding pennies to Cup #2. Drop the pennies into the center of the cup, 1 at a time. This is the lever's effort.

5. Write down what happens after you drop each penny into Cup #2. If nothing happens, write that down, too.
6. Is the lever balanced after adding 5 pennies? If not, add more pennies to Cup #2, one by one.

Conclusion:

How many pennies do you need to balance the load? Was our hypothesis correct? Now let's think of something we can change in this experiment. Maybe we could move the position of the fulcrum. At the moment, it's exactly between the load and the effort, or between Cup #1 and Cup #2.

You might be asking yourself the following question: What would happen if the fulcrum was closer to the load? Let's test this hypothesis: **Less effort is needed to lift the load if it is closer to the fulcrum.** Get ready to experiment again!

Instructions:

1. Empty Cup #2. Make sure there are still 5 pennies in Cup #1.
2. Lay the ruler on the spool so that the fulcrum is at the 3-inch (7.6 cm) mark, which is closer to the load.
3. Now add pennies to Cup #2 one at a time. How many do you need to add this time to lift the load, since the fulcrum has been moved? Be sure to write down your observations!

Move the fulcrum away from the load. What happens?

4. Next, try moving the fulcrum further away from the load by placing it at the 9-inch (22.9 cm) mark. How many pennies do you have to add to balance everything this time? Record your observations once more.

Conclusion:

Does moving the fulcrum closer to Cup #1 mean that fewer pennies are needed to lift the load? Did we prove that the position of the fulcrum affects how easy or hard it is to lift a load? Where should the fulcrum be positioned to make lifting the easiest?

Experiment #2
The Open Door

You probably use levers every day.

You probably figured out in Experiment #1 that a load is easier to move when it's closer to the fulcrum than the effort is. But did that conclusion leave you asking a similar question: Is a load easier to move when the effort is farther from the fulcrum than the load is? Let's figure out the answer by trying to prove this hypothesis: **A load *is* easier to move when the effort is farther away from the fulcrum than the load is.**

Here's what you'll need:

- A hinged door that opens away from you

Sometimes you can experiment with something as simple as a door.

Instructions:

1. Close the door just enough so that it doesn't latch and can be pushed open.
2. Push on the door on the edge closest to the hinges. Can you open it?
3. Close the door and try again. This time, push on the outer edge of the door, which is farthest from the hinges. Is it easier to open the door? Don't forget to write down your observations!

Observations

Conclusion:

You may have already realized that the door is a lever. Now identify the different parts of the lever and where each is positioned. Where is the fulcrum? Where is the load? Your hand pushing on the door is the effort, of course. You changed the position of the effort in this experiment. How did that affect how easy or hard it was to open the door? Did we prove our hypothesis?

Compound levers are machines made up of more than one lever. The different levers are joined at the fulcrum, and each lever helps the other to work. Some examples of compound levers are scissors, nail clippers, and tweezers.

Cutting your own hair with a compound lever might not be a great idea!

Experiment #3

Pull Down to Go Up?

↖ A pulley can make it easier to get water from a well.

What is a pulley? A pulley is a simple machine that is often made up of a wheel that turns on an axle and a rope or cable. The rope passes over the wheel, which can be fitted with grooves to keep the rope from slipping off. One end of the rope is connected to the load. The other end hangs freely and can be pulled.

You can observe pulleys at work all around you. For example, a crane uses a pulley to lift building materials. A pulley at the top of a flagpole lets you raise and lower a flag.

One type of pulley is called a fixed pulley because it stays in a single spot. It helps you lift something up and lower it back down again. With a fixed pulley, the weight of the load is equal to the amount of effort you need to lift it. Because of the effort required, it might seem like it doesn't matter if you use a pulley or not. But it is easier to pull down on a rope than lift up a heavy object.

What if you need to lift a bucket of water? Not too hard, right? You could lift it by the handle with your hands. But what if you need to lift the bucket of water high up over your head? It could get pretty tricky—and messy! And your arms might become tired if you had to hold it up for a long time.

So, ask yourself the following question: Will a fixed pulley help you lift a bucket of water higher over your head than if you weren't using a pulley at all? Let's test this hypothesis: **A fixed pulley *will* make it easier to lift a bucket of water higher over your head than if you weren't using a pulley at all.** Ready to see if you're right?

Here's what you'll need:

- A long piece of rope
- A sturdy tree branch or the top of a swing set
- A bucket filled with water

Try not to get wet!

Instructions:

1. Hold onto one end of the rope. Toss the other end over a tree branch or swing set. Then grab both ends of the rope.
2. Tie one end of the rope to the handle of the bucket.

Pulling down on the rope makes the bucket move in the opposite direction.

3. Pull down on the loose end of the rope. What happens to the bucket? How high can you get the bucket to go? Remember to write down everything you notice.
4. Now pick up the bucket of water with your hands and try to lift it over your head without a pulley. How high were you able to lift the bucket? Write down your observations.

Conclusion:

You may have observed that the top of the tree branch or swing set acted as a fixed pulley. It didn't include a wheel, but the rope could travel freely over it. Were you able to lift the bucket higher with the pulley or without it? Unless you're *really* tall, you were able to lift that bucket higher with the pulley!

Experiment #4
Lighten the Load!

← Movable pulleys can be used to lift heavy objects.

You have learned that a fixed pulley stays in one place. A movable pulley, on the other hand, is attached to a load. As the load moves, this type of pulley shifts up or down with it.

You know that, with a fixed pulley, the amount of effort equals the weight of the load. So, you may be asking yourself the following question: With a movable pulley, do you need to use less effort to lift a heavy load? Let's figure out the answer by testing this hypothesis: **Movable pulleys allow you to use an amount of effort less than the weight of the load.** Now prepare to learn if your hypothesis is correct! For this experiment, you can create your own simple movable pulley with some paper clips and string.

Here's what you'll need:
- 2 chairs
- A yardstick
- Large paper clips
- An object to lift, such as a stuffed animal or a plastic mug (Try to find an object that will be easy to tie string to or that has a handle.)
- Nylon string

The paper clip is a movable pulley—it moves with the load.

Instructions:

1. Place the chairs back-to-back with about 2 feet (0.6 meter) between them. Lay the yardstick across the top of the chairs.
2. A paper clip will act as our pulley. A string will be able to pass through it easily. Tie the paper clip onto the load you want to lift using a small piece of string.
3. Next, cut a long piece of string. Tie one end of the piece of string to the yardstick. Thread the other end through the paper clip pulley on your load.
4. Pull up on the free end of the string to lift your load off the ground. What happens? Write down your observations.

The pulley attached to your load is a movable pulley because it's moving with your load. The movable pulley carries part of the load. Does the rope tied to the yardstick help hold the weight of the load, too? Do you think dividing the weight of the load makes it easier to lift?

Let's go a step further and ask another question: Do more pulleys result in less effort lifting a load? Here are two possible hypotheses to choose from:

Hypothesis #1: The more pulleys you use, the less effort you will need to lift a load.

Hypothesis #2: Using more pulleys will not change the amount of effort you need to lift a load.

1. Keep this experiment set up like the one before, with one end of the rope tied to the yardstick and the other end threaded through your movable pulley. Create a fixed pulley by tying another paper clip onto the yardstick with string.
2. Thread the string through the fixed pulley on the yardstick. Pull down on the free end of the string to lift your load off the ground. Did you need to use as much effort to lift the load as when you were working with only a single pulley? Do more pulleys share the weight of the load? Did you prove that more pulleys decrease the effort you need to lift an object?

Now you have two pulleys!

Conclusion:

Notice how much string you pulled to lift the load in this experiment. You needed to pull the string a longer distance than the load actually moved. We can conclude that the pulleys allowed you to use less effort to lift a heavy load. But you used that effort over a greater distance. So, the amount of work you did was the same.

Experiment #5
Ready to Drive

← Conveyor belts are used in all kinds of factories.

Pulleys aren't just used to lift objects. A drive belt is a type of pulley that causes other pulleys to turn. It features two wheels on axles with a continuous loop of rope—or a belt—between them. Imagine a factory with boxes moving from place to place on a conveyor belt. A pulley on a drive belt called the drive pulley is turned by a motor. The belt makes another pulley turn to create a continuous motion.

Let's create a drive belt of our own and experiment with the way it moves using ribbon spools as pulleys. You may be asking yourself: What will happen when the drive pulley on a drive belt turns? Will the position of the drive belt make a difference in how the other pulley moves? Our hypothesis could be: **The direction the drive pulley turns and the overall position of the drive belt will affect how the other pulley in the belt moves.**

Here's what you'll need:

- A ribbon, about 30 to 36 inches (76 to 91 cm) long
- 2 wooden dowels or skewers (round rods or sticks)
- 2 empty ribbon spools that are about the same size, labeled Spool #1 and Spool #2
- A shoe box or piece of Styrofoam that is about the length and width of a shoe box

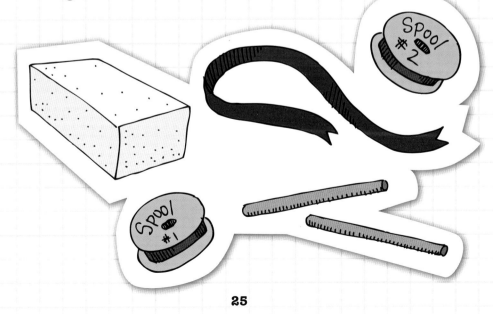

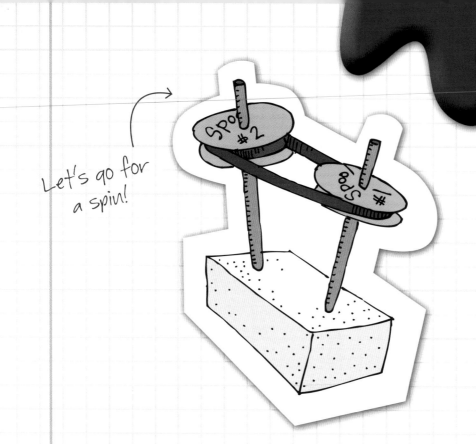

Let's go for a spin!

Instructions:

1. Tie the ends of the piece of ribbon to form a continuous belt.
2. Poke a skewer through the center hole of Spool #1 and into one end of the box or Styrofoam, to hold it steady.
3. Loop the ribbon around Spool #1. Then loop it around Spool #2, and secure this second spool to the box with the other skewer so that it feels tight.
4. Turn Spool #1. What happens to Spool #2? Be sure to notice the direction Spool #2 is turning and how fast it turns. Do the spools spin at the same speed? Does one spin faster? Write down all your observations.

5. Remove one of the skewers so that you can flip that spool over and crisscross the ribbon. Secure it to the box. Turn Spool #1 again. What do you notice about the direction Spool #2 turns?

Conclusion:

What can we conclude about what happens when a drive pulley turns? How does the position of the drive belt affect the pulley's action?

You may hear your parents talk about having to get a belt replaced in their car. Ask an adult if you can look under the hood of the car sometime. Search for the car's driving belt. See if you can spot the pulleys holding the belt in place. Driving belts are often made of rubber. The belt in a car helps run the water pump and power steering.

Experiment #6
Do It Yourself!

↖ Give it a try! You're sure to come up with a lot of ideas about levers and pulleys.

Once you start experimenting with levers and pulleys, you'll come up with more ideas to try. Find a big rock outside. Could you use a lever to lift it?

A wheelbarrow is a type of lever.

load

effort

fulcrum

How long should your lever be? Will you need help from a friend to increase the amount of effort? And where, oh where, should your fulcrum be to make the job easiest?

Next time you step into an elevator, think for a moment. Some elevators operate through a system of pulleys. How might this system lift a box filled with people? How could it be designed to use the least amount of effort to move such a heavy load?

Scientists learn from their experiments and apply what they've learned to new ideas. You don't have to be a muscular superhero to lift a heavy load. With the right tools, a scientist can do the same job!

GLOSSARY

axle (AK-suhl) the central bar around which a wheel turns

conclusion (kuhn-KLOO-zhuhn) a final decision, thought, or opinion

effort (EH-fert) the force that is needed to move a load

fulcrum (FUL-kruhm) the part of a lever that supports the rest of the machine but does not move

hypothesis (hy-POTH-uh-sihss) a logical guess about what will happen in an experiment

load (LODE) something that is being lifted or moved

method (METH-uhd) a way of doing something

observations (ob-zur-VAY-shuhnz) things that are seen or noticed with one's senses

simple machines (SIM-puhl muh-SHEENZ) basic devices that make work easier

FOR MORE INFORMATION

BOOKS

Gardner, Robert. *Sensational Projects with Simple Machines*. Berkeley Heights, NJ: Enslow Elementary, 2006.

Oxlade, Chris. *Levers*. North Mankato, MN: Smart Apple Media, 2008.

Richards, Jon. *Forces & Simple Machines*. New York: PowerKids Press, 2008.

WEB SITES

Edheads: Simple Machines
www.edheads.org/activities/simple-machines/
A variety of activities and experiments related to simple machines

Exploratorium Science Snacks
www.exploratorium.edu/snacks/
Experiments for several different science topics

Planet Science: Levers Made Simple
www.planet-science.com/under11s/index.html?page=/under11s/levers/index.html
Additional information about simple machines, as well as some easy-to-do experiments

INDEX

About the → Author

Dana Meachen Rau loves to observe. Wondering about nature inspires her to write. Researching information helps her answer questions about how the world works, and writing books allows her to share what she has discovered with others. Rau has written more than 200 books for children, many on science topics, for all age levels. She lives, writes, and experiments at home in Burlington, Connecticut.